# BROOKLYN
# MODERN

———

# BROOKLYN MODERN

—

*ARCHITECTURE, INTERIORS & DESIGN*
*DIANA LIND*
PHOTOGRAPHY BY YOKO INOUE

# AESTHETIC IMPROVEMENTS

—

*PART ONE*

# GUT RENOVATIONS

—

*PART TWO*

# NEW WORK

—

*PART THREE*

# INTRODUCTION

*BY DIANA LIND*

"Lateral growth—the social transformation of New York beyond Manhattan—is likely to be the most important urban development in the city for the foreseeable future." So wrote *New York Times* architecture critic Herbert Muschamp in a review of the new entrance to the Brooklyn Museum. That Muschamp had his premonition in April 2004 was, depending on one's perception of the city at that time, either rather overdue or surprisingly prescient.

Noticeable changes in the dynamic between Manhattan and the boroughs were at least a decade in the making by the time Muschamp penned his review. Yet, many Manhattanites hadn't recognized them. So ingrained was Manhattan's predominance that rumors of Brooklyn's new trendiness—epitomized by DUMBO, its very own acronym neighborhood, art galleries and clubs in Williamsburg, and the literati nexus in Park Slope—seemed like the same feeble hype that a decade earlier proclaimed Jersey City and Hoboken the next most promising enclaves of bohemia.

Until the turn of the century, magazines and newspapers rarely reported on New York cultural life beyond Manhattan. But in the past five years, that trend has changed markedly. An unscientific survey of the *New York Times*, for instance, reflects such growing interest: In 2000, the total amount of food and wine articles that mention Brooklyn numbers only 64; the figure for 2006 is more than double. Likewise, the borough's most established cultural institution, the Brooklyn Academy of Music, is referred to the same number of times in the six years between 2000 and 2006 as it is in the 15 years prior.

Whether Manhattanites and the media were late to recognize changes taking place in Brooklyn matters less than what Brooklyn's transformation has meant in terms of an unquantifiable but undeniable disruption of the area's decades-long, low-key status quo. Commercial strips such as Bedford, Atlantic, and Vanderbilt avenues and Smith and Court streets now sprout wine shops instead of bodegas, bistros instead of diners; a brownstone's average price in undervalued areas such as Fort Greene and Boerum Hill has quadrupled in little more than a decade; many traditionally working-class black or Hispanic neighborhoods have been met by an influx of young, white families searching for more space, speculating strategically on real estate or looking to get closer to good public schools.

No doubt, when Muschamp observed the new green-glass, Polshek Partnership–designed museum entrance, he also sensed that the slow shift away from Manhattan's hegemony was not just another fleeting trend. Though Brooklyn's renewed development may have begun as a result of Manhattan's enormous real estate costs, bottleneck traffic, and unconscionable overdevelopment, Muschamp's review highlighted the directedness of the changes taking place across the borough. People were moving or staying there by choice, not by default.

Steven Holl Architects designed this center section for Pratt Institute's Higgins Hall in the Clinton Hill area of Brooklyn. Housing the university's architecture department, the new building also connects two pre-existing buildings (an example of an unrenovated classroom at bottom). Because the building's floor plates didn't quite match up, a ramp joins the levels at each floor. Two skylights facing in opposite directions funnel northern and southern light into the studio spaces (above left). The facade (top), sheathed mostly in inexpensive channel glass, suggests the dissonance created by the uneven floorplates inside. The building receives plentiful daylight and glows at night.

The last time Brooklyn inspired noteworthy architecture was about 150 years ago, when the borough, then mostly farmland, was transformed into blocks of brownstones.

Initially designed as an inexpensive alternative to the townhouses cropping up in Manhattan, the brownstone has since come to define the borough. Brownstone structure is highly influenced by the Dutch, who first colonized the area and who were accustomed to building structures that could tolerate flooding. Brownstones keep the Dutch *stoep* (stoop) and dual entrances on the ground and parlor floors. This basic form has given way to a divergence of styles, as architects and homeowners implemented features inspired by the structures of ancient Greece and Italian palazzos (in the Greek Revival and Italianate styles popular during the middle of the 19th century).

But what really differentiated the brownstone from its townhouse sisters was the use of its namesake material. Brownstone was a cheap substitute for classic materials such as granite, limestone, and marble, and some architects even created brick townhouses that used brownstone for the trim only. It's worth noting that brownstone reflected the houses' intended inhabitants: the growing middle class. As Walt Whitman once wrote, "Our architectural greatness consists in the hundreds and thousands of superb private dwellings, for the comfort and luxury of the great body of middle class people—a kind of architecture unknown until comparatively late times and no where known to such an extent as in Brooklyn." Whitman was right: These were superb places to live in then, and what seems most miraculous is how well the structures have withstood centuries of wear.

To further lower costs, residents, not architects, found ways to make the brownstone even less expensive. Beginning in the 20th century, for example, many brownstone owners converted the servants' quarters on the ground floor into profitable rental units. By the 1960s and 1970s, many of Brooklyn's upper and middle class residents had relocated to the suburbs, and brownstones were frequently divided into single-room-occupancy dwellings (SROs). In a true measure of how much Brooklyn has changed since those times, an increasing number of residents are returning these multifamily houses to single-family homes.

The brownstone has also encouraged the casual, residential life that has flourished in Brooklyn. That's due in part to a brownstone's scale and style, which encourage a sense of community. Two-family homes require a reliance on neighbors to pay the rent; such a relationship connects owners to their tenants in a personal way that is rare in Manhattan. The backyard provides opportunities for personal connection, through its sense of shared space. Although the gardens of brownstones are neatly separated, one can still see, hear, and smell one's neighbors. And unlike Manhattan, where buildings might stand 40 stories tall, a very small percentage of Brooklynites live more than five stories up. The

Polshek Partnership is responsible for an extensive, 25-year plan for renovating the Brooklyn Museum on Eastern Parkway. Originally designed by McKim, Mead & White, the building suffered a period of neglect during the middle of the 20th century.

In 2004, Polshek Partnership completed the first phase of renovation, which included the entry pavillion, public plaza, and outdoor exhibition and performance spaces.

With its blue-green glass suggesting transparency, the new entrance revitalized the building's image.

realities of living within such an enclave attracts a specific population: those more interested in the extended family provided by a brownstone community, as opposed to the converted industrial buildings in DUMBO and Williamsburg, which provide a degree of isolation similar to an apartment building.

To build or to renovate in Brooklyn is then to understand the brownstone's modest heritage: its narrow proportions, close quarters, and earthy materials.

For decades now, a humble approach to American architecture has been categorically denied. Projects that attract the media's attention—boldly-designed museums, stadiums, apartment towers, and university buildings—are fashioned with gobs of money. At once they convey their patrons' wealth and their designers' egos. These super-projects have turned architects into "starchitects"—a name that underscores such projects' lack of earthly context.

But recently, Brooklyn has produced a spate of architectural projects that seems remarkably different from what is shown in the mainstream media. Here architects and clients struggle with the innate difficulties of renovating antiquated brownstones and buildings. These buildings are often literally recycled, and in the case of Bill Harvey's home (page 180) make use of salvaged materials, appliances, and furnishings.

These architects and homeowners choose to contend with the brownstone's narrow rectangular shape, rather than defy it. Renovations such as Jordan Parnass's split-plane layout (page 84) and Noroof Architects' duplex (page 76) enlarge the sense of space without adding square feet.

Unlike the second homes and beach getaways found in shelter magazines, the houses in this book and around Brooklyn are primary residences, home to owners who plan to live in them for a good part of their lives. That fact accounts for the clever renovation of homes like Perla Delson's (page 24), completed not for vanity's sake or resale value, but with an eye toward enhancing daily life.

Likewise, the architects featured here have made efforts to introduce environmentally sustainable products into their designs. Coggan Crawford Schaut (opposite) and Susan Boyle and Benton Brown (page 130) are specifically in the business of eco-friendly design. Many other architects have shown a concern for the urban environment by adding to the density of the city with their infill construction.

Lastly, while the work here has some glamour to it, one can't help but notice that one of the most exciting aspects of the brownstone is its facade, which is designed for pedestrians to admire. The exteriors created by Christian Hubert (page 110) and David Adjaye (page 160) enliven the cityscape, strutting their modernism and engaging the public at the same time.

These elements point to a style so often missing from our conception of modern architecture. Even publications that proclaim to show how people

As Brooklyn real estate has grown more desirable, new condominium developments have sprung up in every neighborhood. Coggan Crawford Schaut, an architecture practice based in Brooklyn, design environmentally sustainable condos like the one above (located in Greenwood Heights). Their work has received awards from the Brooklyn AIA and the Energy Star seal of approval.

In this project, local fly-ash concrete, rapidly renewable woods, super-efficient appliances, low-flow showers, VOC-free paints, and fluorescent lighting all contributed to energy efficiency and exhibited the firm's environmental conscience.

"really live" tend to avoid the compromises required to make a home within tight budgets and tight spaces. As befits the Brooklyn ethos, this book presents houses that are all owned or designed by young people who value good architecture and design, but who couldn't or didn't want to throw money at design challenges. Rather than brush over financial constraints, I examine them to show how deftly a new generation of architects and designers has developed inexpensive solutions to economic realities.

Likewise, by and large these houses are presented as they looked when photographer Yoko Inoue and I showed up to shoot them. Unlike the staging done for most magazines —where everyday linens are swapped for crisper-looking ones, artworks deployed to make a non-collector seem savvy, and books added to previously bare shelves—we have left these spaces largely untouched. There is mess in some corners; papers that need to be filed; open closets and refrigerators.

In the course of writing the book, I referred to architects and clients by their first names. I hoped doing so would endear readers to this friendly community of architects, designers, and homeowners. First-person essays by local bloggers Grace Bonney of Design*Sponge and Jonathan Butler of Brownstoner describe the evolution of Brooklyn style and brownstone renovations, respectively.

New residential architecture projects aren't the sole ventures of significance in Brooklyn. Large development projects such as the Atlantic Yards complex, rezoned neighborhoods that allow for large condominium and commercial towers, and new shopping centers have garnered attention for their size and impact on the community. But little attention is given to the many small commercial, civic, and institutional projects whose aesthetics define "Brooklyn architecture." Some of them lack architectural merit; others are quite handsome and are produced with the same spirit of economy and community as the residences presented here. Robert Ivy, critic and editor of *Architectural Record*, contributes an essay on the changing face of Brooklyn.

Now may be the time for an assessment of the architectural upheaval felt across Brooklyn. While many of the architects and homeowners that I interviewed for the book felt that a study of new architecture in Brooklyn is long overdue, the body of work still feels young to me. Yet, as I selected which projects to publish, I realized that *Brooklyn Modern* was not meant to be an all-inclusive retrospective as so many surveys claim to present. Brooklyn is changing—has even changed since these photographs were taken and will have changed again by the time you read these words—and an effort to capture all the residences that have contributed something new to the borough would fall flat. Instead, the projects published here are case studies in a style of urban living replicated throughout cities across the United States. By publishing these projects now, I hope to encourage local architects to create sustainable architecture for this city—and for many more cities across the country.

Long Island University's Brooklyn campus is slowly undergoing an architectural transformation. This 110,000-square-foot gymnasium (above), designed by Miami–based architecture firm Arquitectonica, exemplifies the university's interest in combining education with architecture. The state-of-the-art facility not only provides a varied recreation space and a home for the LIU Blackbirds basketball team, but allows the health sciences program to have a teaching practicum there with a local hospital.

# AESTHETIC IMPROVEMENTS

—

*PART ONE*

HOW TO CREATE AN AESTHETICALLY PLEASING SPACE OUT OF A DARK, NARROW BROWNSTONE INTERIOR? THIS CHALLENGE CAN OFTEN FEEL LIKE PLAYING WITH A RUBIK'S CUBE. THERE ARE SO MANY ARCHITECTURAL CONSTRAINTS PROVIDED BY THE BROWNSTONE FORM THAT THE EASIEST AND MOST OFTEN USED RESPONSE THROUGHOUT BROOKLYN IS TO REPLICATE FLOORPLANS, PANCAKE-STYLE, OVER THREE OR FOUR STORIES. WHEN ARCHITECTS, CLIENTS, AND HOMEOWNERS DISCUSS RENOVATIONS THEN, THE MAIN QUESTION THEY USUALLY ASK IS NOT HOW TO REPACKAGE THIS LAYOUT, BUT JUST HOW MUCH ORIGINAL DETAIL ARE WE KEEPING AND WHAT COLORS ARE WE PAINTING THE WALLS?

A MORE INTERESTING APPROACH WOULD BE: HOW DO WE REPURPOSE SPACES FOR THE WAYS THAT 21ST–CENTURY FAMILIES LIVE? IN THESE FIVE HOUSES, ALL ORIGINALLY BUILT MORE THAN A CENTURY AGO, THEIR SPATIAL FLOW HAS BEEN ENTIRELY RECONSIDERED BY THE OWNERS, ARCHITECTS, AND FRIENDS. AS A RESULT, A SPACE THAT ONCE WAS A BATHROOM BECOMES A KITCHEN, OR A BEDROOM BECOMES A LIVING ROOM. CLEVER USE OF INTERIOR DECORATING (PAINT, MATERIALS, ETC.) ASSIGNS A FAR MORE MODERN IDENTITY THAN THEIR PRESERVED EXTERIORS WOULD SUGGEST. THESE KINDS OF INTERVENTIONS SHOW A NUANCED QUESTIONING OF THE MEANING OF TRADITIONAL DETAIL—MOLDINGS AREN'T SACRED HERE, INNOVATION IS.

# PERLA DELSON

Perla Delson and her husband Maitland Jones had been looking for a brownstone for a year and a half when they finally bought a building that was collapsing into the street. Originally a church, the building required so many architectural interventions to rehabilitate it that many buyers were wary of the place. "The real estate market wasn't moving in this neighborhood at the time. And typically people want outside space," Perla says, explaining why the brownstone was such a steal.

After enduring a rigorous landmarks process, Perla had to rebuild 60 of 75 feet of one of the walls (the building measures 34-by-75 feet), add heavy timbers to support the roof, and then contend with dividing up a space whose volume seems infinitely larger than its square footage. Perla chose to create an apartment for a rent-paying tenant; she had turned down opportunities to buy other buildings because, as an architect who loves those old houses, it was emotionally difficult to divide up the space. Here, she was able to reconfigure without regret. The building, once used as a warehouse and then a church, had been vacant for some time and thus presented a blank slate.

As a result, the interior renovation focuses on shared spaces and max-imizing architectural innovation by using inexpensive materials. The double—or triple?—height dining area, equipped with a 20-foot-long dining table made by her husband from plain IKEA wooden planks, allows for plenty of uses beyond dinner parties. Behind the table is an enormous set of custom bookshelves, paid for by bartering architectural services with local cabinet maker, Stephen Reinert of Polygon Projects. More fun than fancy, the kitchen cabinets are made of 13-ply Baltic birch with a colorized finish surface perfect for a young family of five. This same plywood material is used throughout the house, in bookcases upstairs and in some of the furniture in the children's rooms.

"One of our concerns when we bought the place was light," Perla says, but you wouldn't guess that from walking through the space. In fact, small doses of eye-popping color balance out the muted gray floors, creating a unique combination of colors. Upstairs, a large wooden cabinet for storing clothes and other items is painted bright yellow and divides the upstairs den from three small bedrooms. These smart, cozy rooms value their privacy, playfully contrasting with the sophisticated main volume below.

opposite: *Architect Perla Delson and her husband (also an architect, Maitland Jones) had been looking to buy a brownstone in Brooklyn for a while when they found a building that had been used as a church. With its enormous volume, the building was suited to modern architectural interventions. Now, the building has a tenant's unit and shelters Perla's family of five.*

left and top right:
*The kitchen features birch wood cabinetry and stainless steel elements. It's funct-ional and colorful, ceding attention to the double-height dining area. The small dining table is designed by Perla's father.*

bottom right:
*The downstairs guest bathroom sleekly hides a shower. Its hexagonal tiles recall the tiles in one of Perla's child-hood friend's houses—they're also an inexpensive tile option. With a*

*glitzy mirror and sink, they add a bit of drama to the space.*

above: *When Perla rebuilt the exterior wall of the house, she enlarged its windows to ensure enough natural light indoors. The bright light allows for muted, gray-painted floorboards and neutral-colored furniture.*

next spread: *Perla bartered architectural services for the custom bookshelves behind the 20-foot-long table, a piece fabricated by her husband from IKEA planks.*

*Aesthetic Improvements*

above: *Upstairs,
more custom
cabinets multitask as
bookshelves, storage
spaces, and desks.
Bins are more practical
for storing a lot of stuff,
Perla says, and so
she uses them instead
of drawers.*

*Aesthetic Improvements*

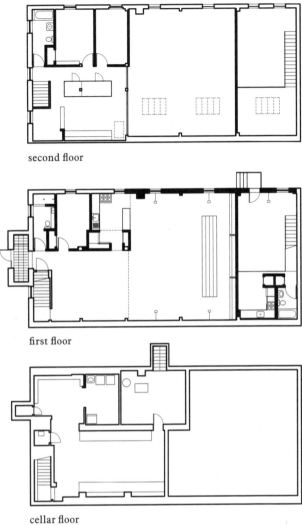

second floor

first floor

cellar floor

left: *The bedrooms are all simple, small spaces as the house prioritizes shared space. The master bedroom keeps everything pared down—a bed, a beam, a piece of art, and a chair create a peaceful composition.*

right: *A floorplan shows the layout of the family's duplex, as well as the way the building is split between owner and rental units.*

# PILAR GUZMÀN, CHRIS MITCHELL & TYLER HAYS

*PARK SLOPE*

opposite: *Pilar and Chris had been living in Chelsea when they saw this Park Slope brownstone one weekend. While the bones of the Victorian were beautiful, the interior needed to be renovated in such a way that would respect and restore the brownstone's traditional details while answering to the couple's modern aesthetics.*

There are people who come to Brooklyn by design and those who do so by accident. Pilar Guzmàn and Chris Mitchell are the latter. "We didn't even know what Park Slope was," Chris says, only half joking. One winter weekend in 2003, when the couple was living in Chelsea with their newborn son, they "discovered" Brooklyn. By the following Monday, they had bought a house there.

What they bought was a 20-foot-wide Victorian brownstone with parquet floors and moldings largely intact. Everything else required renovation. "It needed so much work—which was precisely what made it affordable. But the last thing we wanted to do was pay for someone else's renovation," Pilar recalls.

Purchasing the house made economic sense. It also fit the couple's personal needs: Pilar and Chris hoped to share the brownstone with Chris's brother, Gregg, and his wife, Andrea. Here, Pilar and Chris's family (two kids and an frequently visiting grandmother) sprawls in a spacious triplex. Gregg and Andrea live in the charming garden apartment.

To execute the renovation, the family reached out to their friend Tyler Hays, owner of the furniture and design company BDDW. Their collaboration resulted in a fantastic renovation: The parlor floor is the public space with an open-plan kitchen, den, and dining area; the second and third floors are dedicated to living and sleeping quarters with small amendments to rooms, such as the creation of a sleeping nook in the den, that personalize the design; and the top floor hosts Chris and Pilar's master suite and master bath.

The traditional elements of the brownstone, such as wood floors and dark wood moldings, remained untouched for tradition's sake. But the building's historicist bent was at odds with the couple's modernist leanings. Custom-built pieces, such as the kitchen island that Chris and Tyler designed and the built-in shelving in the family room, update the spaces. "Choosing materials was about keeping to the look of a mahogany brownstone," Tyler says. "It was really answering to the home, and using materials that didn't compete: Carrera marble, mahogany, walnut."

The project began in 2004, and during the renovation, Chris and Pilar lived in a variety of places—from their pad in Chelsea to a sublet on Second Street in Brooklyn (which served as an introduction to the neighborhood) to a friend's vacant apartment. But in the end, in spite of all the moving, the process was worth it. "For all the money in the world, we wouldn't move back to Manhattan," Pilar says.

*Aesthetic Improvements*

left and right:
*Because Pilar
and Chris felt that
destroying the
brownstone's original
details would be
sacrilege, the couple
modernized the space
with furniture, art,
and a clean palette
of colors.*

left: *When looking for a brownstone, the couple was interested in a building large enough to accomodate living with Chris's younger brother Gregg and his wife, Andrea. Pilar's mother also is a frequent guest. The house's tone is* casual and reflects these familial connections.

right: *Original details that Pilar and Chris were reluctant to remove include impeccable parquet floors.*

this page: *For the parlor floor, Tyler Hays of BBDW created a custom kitchen island out of wood and carrera marble. Old glass doors were reused as kitchen cabinets. The kitchen accesses a backyard patio.*

opposite: *The parlor floor is dedicated to public spaces and the kitchen flows into a den which abuts the dining area.*

*Aesthetic Improvements*

*Aesthetic Improvements*

previous spread: *The master bedroom is a pure white space. Tyler suggested painting the brick wall behind the bed white in order to keep the room filled with light.*

opposite: *The master bath receives sunlight from a skylight cut out of the roof. Marble subway tiles continue the palette from the parlor floor.*

above: *Custom bookshelves minimize clutter and maximize style.*

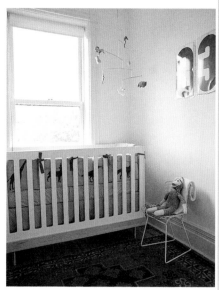

left and right: *Pilar edits the parenting lifestyle magazine,* Cookie, *and thus her kids' rooms are laboratories for the magazine.*

above: *In the case
of the elder son's
room, retro modern
meets tradition with
Marimekko quilt,
wooden sleigh bed,
and BDDW rug.*

# GREGORY MERRYWEATHER

"This project was mostly about demolition—removing things, not adding them," says Greg Merryweather regarding the renovation of his home. "We targeted the money on the kitchen and tried to use what was here opportunistically. There wasn't a lot of architectural character to the house, and that was an advantage because there was nothing to work around." The building, formerly used as a copy shop that catered to nearby Pratt Institute, was in good structural shape. As a result, the low-cost renovation, estimated at about $100 per square foot, allowed Greg, his wife, Anna, and their son to move in just four months after demolition began.

For this charming house, which was built at the same time as the identical one next door, Greg didn't have a preconceived architectural plan. "I definitely have an architectural manifesto, but I wouldn't want to live in it," he says. Instead, he and Anna, a magazine editor, created a livable home that is suited to their needs. From wooden-beamed ceilings to newly laid floors, the house is stripped of excess detail. The money was well spent in the kitchen because Anna, who has worked for cooking icons Alice Waters and Martha Stewart, enjoys passing a lot of time there. Smaller touches, such as the addition of a storage cube in the master bedroom, show that the couple prioritizes the practical. The interior decorating—a mixture of vintage 20th-century finds—is also sensitive to budget: "Most of the stuff here was bought on eBay," says Greg, pointing to a few objects like the hanging school-style lamps and the Arne Jacobsen chairs.

Usually, architects love designing their own houses because personal projects allow them to take a carte blanche approach. But Greg notes, "It's a lot of fun working with a client; it's a symbiosis where neither owner nor architect gets exactly what he wants. The result is a little resistance and texture." Greg has worked on a number of other brownstones in the neighborhood that required greater rehabilitation (including Christian Hubert's project, page 110) and a ground-up condominium project in Williamsburg.

How to define the area's architecture is still up in the air, according to Greg. "That there is a new Brooklyn architecture is a very recent phenomenon. It's pretty incredible if the BAM cultural center and a few of the other big projects go up. Fifteen years ago, no one would have thought this would happen."

opposite: *This cute, two-story house is unusual for Clinton Hill, a neighborhood better known for its grand mansions. Formerly a copy shop near Pratt Institute, the house only needed a modest renovation of the interior. The exterior is enlivened by light blue trim around the windows.*

left: *The interior renovation mostly involved removing elements rather than adding ones. Greg found many furnishings—such as these Kofod-Larsen chairs—on eBay.*

right and opposite: *Original banisters and parquet floors were salvaged upsairs, while downstairs, beams were kept exposed and new flooring had to be installed.*

opposite: *The upstairs features three small bedrooms, one of which serves as Greg's office.*

above: *The bedroom features the only addition to the house—a large closet space. The chartreuse wall paint mimics Pratt Institute's leafy, green quad and sculpture garden across the street.*

above: *Anna is an editor for a food and lifestyle magazine, so Greg was intent on creating a spacious, open kitchen where she could cook.*

right: *The backyard area accommodates the family's herb and vegetable garden.*

# 1100
# ARCHITECT

This house is one of three Greek Revival brownstones built for a merchant's daughters in the mid-19th century. Twenty-five-feet-wide, the brownstone had many of its original details intact when its owners bought it, but was dark and not living up to its potential. The owners—a couple with two children—had a very specific idea of what kind of renovation they needed. The husband hails from Los Angeles, and he wanted the house filled with as much natural light as possible; otherwise, the couple hoped to restore original details such as staircase banisters, wooden floors, and moldings.

In commissioning 1100 Architect to renovate the house, the owners sought to radically update the brownstone by increasing its indoor-outdoor connection—a luxury that is so rare in New York City. By opening the house's back extension, a domino effect of modifications to the interior resulted. On both the parlor floor level and the ground floor, the walls of the extension were replaced with glass. As a result, natural light flows from the back of the house all the way to the front and creates an airiness that defies the cramped feeling inside most brownstones. Usually a dreary level, the ground floor is now open to nature and a beautiful backyard garden. Using 4-inch-square tiles to pave the floor of the extension and the backyard (an element the client requested after being inspired by a Carlo Scarpa building in Italy), the office/sitting room is integrated with the garden.

"We always like to push the envelope, but be conscious and respectful of existing physical conditions," says Juergen Riehm, the architect. Indeed, what makes this five-story house such a success is that neither form nor function overwhelms the other. For example, the extension is transformed from just a practical spatial addition into something of a jewel-box, with its facade paneled in Italian limestone. While a neutral color, the material possesses a pleasing horizontal grain pattern. Likewise, the green roof atop the extension serves to absorb rainwater and add a little oxygen back to the air, but it also furthers the house's complimentary color scheme of browns, greens, and whites with its combination of wood, grass, and tile.

Inside, a better sense of spatial flow and appropriate scale dictated creating larger openings between the main living spaces on the first floor, modernizing details such as oxidized metal on staircase balustrades, and custom cabinetry that hide sliding doors, bathrooms, and storage. Surprisingly, rather than call attention to themselves, these elements serve to highlight the original architecture.

opposite: *This Greek Revival brownstone in Brooklyn Heights was radically transformed when the architects replaced an existing extension to the building with a modern, glass enclosure. On the bottom two levels, the interior of the house is filled with light streaming in from the extension, while a green roof sits nicely on top of the extension.*

left: *The architects further connected the indoors with the outdoor garden by replacing the extension's solid walls with glass. They also used similar paving stones indoors as the ones in the garden outdoors.*

right: *The staircase exemplifies the architects' ability to merge old and new. The original banisters sit atop new storage space. When the drawers are shut, they present a seamless front.*

opposite: *In the upstairs den, traditional moldings are modernized with bold furnishings and new bookshelves.*

left and right:
*The owners of the
brownstone were
very concerned with
making the house feel
light and airy. The
above two photographs
demonstrate how
the glass extension
floods the whole first
floor with sunlight.*

above: *The dining
room has access to
the garden through
a new staircase located
just behind double
glass doors. The
owners' impressive
art collection includes
works by Richard
Serra, John Baldesari,
and other artists.*

opposite and right:
*Located on the second
floor, the master
bedroom is enhanced
by a new green roof
planted on top of the
extension. The green
roof absorbs rain runoff
and adds a little oxygen
back to the air.*

left: *The master bath
echoes the colors of the
green roof. As in all the
bathrooms of the house,
here the mirror is inset
and backlit.*

# LENA
# CORWIN

*FORT GREENE*

"We just had a feeling it was right and took a little bit of a leap of faith," says Lena Corwin about the decision to buy a brownstone in Fort Greene. Sounds simple enough. Indeed, for Lena—a textile designer, illustrator, and blogger— the harrowing adventure of renovating a brownstone with her husband, Josh, was made easier by working slowly on cosmetic changes to her own duplex apartment, while saving the upstairs rental units for a renovation at a later date.

*Glamour* magazine also expedited the process when they gave her apartment a makeover. The magazine team helped by painting the rooms neutral, contrasting colors that play up the brownstone's traditional details and highlight the apartment's to-die-for ceiling heights. Other tips included painting window frames to match moldings, extending an area rug to under-neath all the living room furniture, and investing in art. Lena very much wanted to live in an old building, and so here in the apartment, moldings and original pocket doors call attention to themselves, but when contrasted with modern furniture, seem not to signify a 19th-century style.

Throughout the house, Lena plays with old and new. Much of the furniture in the house came from Lena's grandmother. "It's really fun to recover old-fashioned furniture with modern fabrics," Lena notes.

As a designer who has worked for style icons Calvin Klein and Jill Stuart, Lena imbues the house with a personal style that is uniquely her own. For example, she decided to put thrift-store plates that were used at her wedding along the wall—an eccentric choice, but one that gives definition to the wall area. Like the products she creates or blogs about, the aesthetic is funky and sweet, but not too precious.

Downstairs, a guest bedroom functions as Lena's studio and a kitchen leads to the backyard. With *Glamour*'s help, she painted kitchen cabinets and walls bright patterns, but sees the design as a temporary fix until she can re-do the whole space. For sure, Lena's new solution will be, like the rest of the house, far from dull.

opposite: *Lena Corwin and her husband, Josh, bought a brownstone in Fort Greene in 2005, renting out the upstairs while living in the lower duplex. The building was structurally sound and required only a minimal, cosmetic renovation to update the interiors.*

left and right: *By using rich, contrasting hues of paint, Lena makes the traditional moldings look novel. Her style is improvised, as exemplified by piling some books under the couch to support it where a leg fell* off. *The painting by Elizabeth Schuppe brings together all the colors in the room.*

opposite: Glamour *magazine asked Lena to "make-over" her apartment. In doing so, they helped pay for the cost of painting and a few decorative elements. Though not designed by Lena, the wallpaper* looks like it could be another one of her beautiful crafts.

*Lena Corwin*

*Aesthetic Improvements*

opposite: *Plates from Lena and Josh's wedding line the staircase going down to the apartment's garden level.*

left and right: *The rustic plank floors and vintage parlor doors add a nice counterpoint to the bold floral bedding.*

left and opposite: *The ground level features a guest bedroom, which serves as Lena's studio. The kitchen and a lovely backyard patio round out the garden floor.*

right: *While not totally satisfied with the outcome of her bright orange kitchen, Lena is holding off on redoing the space until she can pull together a more thorough kitchen renovation.*

# EVERYDAY STYLE

*BY GRACE BONNEY*

When I first moved to Brooklyn in 2003, I would ride the G, L, and F trains between Williamsburg, Park Slope, Fort Greene, DUMBO, and Carroll Gardens, checking out local shops like The Future Perfect, Matter, and Spring to get a taste of what local artists were up to. But over the past four years these stores have changed from local favorites to international design destinations. Brooklyn artists and designers have become trendsetters on a larger scale, no longer famous to a few, but instead synonymous with cutting-edge style around the globe.

I'll never forget picking up Lorena Barrezueta's Gourmet Dishware collection at The Future Perfect and being struck by the sense of playfulness and irony that went into each piece. Lorena, then a recent Parsons School of Design graduate, had cast take-out containers to make porcelain dishware that she then glazed or finished with gold detailing. While it may seem commonplace now, her idea of honoring disposable, or even "cheap" materials and products seemed like such a novel approach to design.

After discovering Lorena's work, I stumbled upon companies such as Redstr/Collective, Scrapile, Jason Miller Studio, and Lite Brite Neon. While the medium and style of their work was as diverse as reclaimed wooden furniture, ceramic antler chandeliers, chairs made from rubber stoppers and whimsical neon lighting fixtures, each studio sent a message that would turn out to be uniquely Brooklyn. Each artist was championing the everyday, that which is familiar to us in an urban environment, and reusing it in a way that has inspired consumers to look at design from a fresh perspective.

Local designers, as well as local art students who attend Pratt, Parsons, FIT, and SVA began exhibiting and selling products that either reused local, easily collected materials (plastic bottles, found wood, construction waste, plastic tubing) or re-imagined familiar designs in a contemporary way. One of the best examples of the latter came from designer Jason Miller. Miller's Subordinated Antler Lamps (now synonymous with the Brooklyn design scene), made of porcelain antlers painted in colors like shocking hot pink, managed to make even *the idea* of an antler chandelier seem cool and cutting edge.

Whether an individual product sparked this design movement or the Brooklyn zeitgeist finally hit its stride, an overall aesthetic created by these local artists started to creep into the look of many homes across the borough. Dining tables from Scrapile, which like all their work are made of materials that were discarded, repurposed, and recovered, and rugs designed by Redstr/Collective that were created from scraps of fabric from a fashion show cropped up in apartments as Brooklynites absorbed and inspired the love of all things found, reclaimed, and reinvented.

I first knew Brooklyn style had hit the big time when I started to hear shop owners on the West Coast promoting the fact that they carried the "Brooklyn look" in their stores. I thought to myself: People care about the Brooklyn look?

Those of us immersed in the aesthetic thought of it as second nature, and the idea that people at the other end of the U.S. (or as far away as Europe) would care about what we were doing over here seemed bizarre. But as the borough's designers grew in popularity, it started to make sense to me—this was a look that was accessible and recognizable. These were products and designs that contained materials and patterns we'd seen before—just presented in a fresh, modern way. The accessibility of Brooklyn style comes from its love of appreciating the commonplace, things familiar by traditional standards. You don't need to empty your house and sell your belongings to afford the look—in fact, it's a look that inspires you to work with what you already have around you.

# GUT
# RENOVATIONS

———

*PART TWO*

*WHILE A MODEST RENOVATION WILL SUFFICE FOR MANY BROOKLYN BROWNSTONES, SOMETIMES THE POSSIBILITY OF SALVAGING THE INTERIOR OF A BUILDING IS STRUCTURALLY IMPOSSIBLE OR AESTHETICALLY UNAPPEALING. THAT'S WHY "GUT RENOVATION" HAS BECOME PART OF THE BOROUGH'S PARLANCE. WHAT IT REALLY MEANS IS KEEPING THE STRUCTURE'S SHELL AND NOT MUCH ELSE. THE PROJECTS HERE DEMONSTRATE VARYING APPROACHES TO SUCH A MAJOR UNDERTAKING.*

*IN MANY WAYS, THE DANCE BETWEEN MODERN AND TRADITIONAL AESTHETICS REPRESENTS THE MAJOR ARCHITECTURAL CONFLICT IN BROOKLYN TODAY. IN LANDMARK AREAS, OR THOSE THAT LOOK AS THOUGH THEY COULD BE, MANY HOMEOWNERS RENOVATE THEIR HOUSES IN A MODERN FASHION INSIDE. BUT FEW OF THESE PROJECTS CREATE A FACADE THAT MATCHES THE INTERIOR—AND THAT INDICATES TO PASSERSBY WHAT THE BUILDING LOOKS LIKE INSIDE. IT'S ONLY WHEN ARCHITECTS HAVE THE LIBERTY TO EXPRESS THEIR MODERNISM ON THE EXTERIOR THAT THEY CAN CREATE SUCH PUBLIC ART FOR PEDESTRIANS.*

# NOROOF
# ARCHITECTS

opposite: *Noroof
Architects purchased
this house shortly after
9/11 and were planning
to do a standard
renovation. However,
once the bare bones
of the structure were
revealed, the architects
created a design that
revolves around a
beautiful tree in their
front yard. On a fall
day, sun filters through
the tree's leaves and
dapples the building's
facade.*

"When we started looking for a place, we really wanted a condo or loft. A brownstone seemed like too much," says Scott Oliver, one half of Noroof Architects. "We're realists," adds Margarita McGrath, the firm's other half. But when the couple found this frame house, they realized that they could manage a modest renovation of it on their own. The two chose to keep half of the building for themselves and to dedicate the back of the house to a tenant.

They planned to renovate only as necessary: fix the roof and maybe punch out a south-facing clerestory window. But as demolition began, revealing beautiful beams and handmade brick, the couple went ahead and gutted the structure until it looked "like a Nepalese tea house," Scott says. According to Margarita, the two "wanted to be able to see the character of the existing structure. And that's what ended up deciding the floor plan."

The 1,000-square-foot building is divided into an 600-square-foot duplex (along with an additional partial height office at the basement level) and a 400-square-foot rental. The first floor contains a bedroom with custom storage units that the couple made themselves. The two couldn't find a storage system that worked with their budget, so, given their desire to challenge their design capabilities, they created furniture from off-the-rack materials. Their platform bed, for instance, is made from two solid-core doors from Home Depot. Plywood and metal form the shelving units. With a local mill worker and welder, they constructed small moving closets for their wardrobes.

The second-level floorplan includes dining, living, cooking, and bathing spaces and an additional sleeping area above the kitchen/bathroom core. Much like houses in Japan (a nominal influence on the house's design), this one relies on maximizing every nook. Margarita and Scott also looked to the natural world for cues regarding the orientation of spaces and windows. Viewed from the yard, a large tree frames the architecture. But from inside, windows provide equal vignettes of tree and streetscape. A deck built on top of the downstairs rental is used for barbecues and relaxing. A sleek wooden container on the ground floor is designed for holding trash, a garden hose, and tools.

For the facade, the couple kept the house's original siding. "The siding keeps the house from looking like too much of an architectural statement," Margarita says. Yet looking at the house from the street, at the light dappling the house's interior, the architecture betrays just how carefully thought-out the project was.

above: *Margarita
and Scott hired a
local welder to create
a staircase they
designed. A simple
ladder leads to a
basement-level office.*

above: *Using stock materials, Margarita and Scott fashioned their own prototypes for storage, such as this sleek, sliding set of drawers.*

right: *The staircase leads to the second floor where the original brick was left exposed.*

previous spread and above: *The second floor features a kitchen, full bathroom, and then free form space. Given the 400-square-foot floorplate, Margarita and Scott kept furnishings minimal and again designed their own storage.*

opposite: *A sleeping loft was deftly inserted a simple, stainless steel kitchen, which has access to a backyard patio.*

# JORDAN PARNASS

opposite: *From
the exterior, the
house looks like just
another Boerum Hill
townhouse were it not
for customized cast
ironwork that hints at
the drastic renovation
inside. The house was
in poor shape when
the architect Jordan
Parnass and his wife,
artist Melanie Crean,
bought it. Like a lot
of young couples buying
their first brownstone,
the purchase coincided
with starting a family.
Jordan had to have the
place renovated in time
for the birth of their son.*

The formulaic floorplans found in nearly every Brooklyn brownstone or town-house can be such a drag. This must have been what Jordan Parnass was thinking when he opted to gut-renovate a dilapidated three-story brick townhouse and fill it with floating floor planes and vertical openings. What was once three stories with a basement, he reconfigured into four light-filled levels, and in the process removed everything except the building's facade, two party walls, roof, and a parlor floor marble mantel.

In a square-foot-conscious city, it was a daring decision to value negative space. While the house has 2,000 useable square feet, it also boasts an unquant-ifiable amount of open-air volume. This way, Jordan maximized the connections within the different floors of the house and between the indoors and out; an expan-siveness results that even a larger house couldn't match.

And within those four floors, every single inch of the house serves a purpose— a kitchen wall doubles as a spice rack, a motorized projection screen is hidden in the parlor-floor ceiling, and most impressively, the basement is converted into a guest bedroom and an office for Jordan's wife, Melanie Crean, an installation artist whose work incorporates video, computer graphics, and sound. Here, Jordan poured radiant concrete flooring and opened this ground floor to the three upstairs levels through a vertical void that reaches from the office to the roof. The space is illuminated by natural light streaming through the glass wall facing the backyard where one can see the Alejandro Bron sculpture located just outside. A clever alignment of Melanie's office two floors below Jordan's own desk space allows husband and wife to see and talk to each other as they sit at opposite ends of the house. French doors separate the office from a lounge area (read: pull-out couch and bar) which serves as a guest bedroom.

This intense customization turned a generic space into a house that tells the story of Jordan and Melanie's taste and identities. Clearly one of their priorities was to fill their home with pieces of art and furniture that spoke to their aesthetics and needs. An 18-foot digital mural by Tali Hinkis of the digital arts group LoVid, was made specifically for the dining area. Work by Barbara Kruger and furniture by the Bourellec brothers grace the main living areas. While the floating, split-level floors, black-painted steel banisters, and brightly colored powder coated surfaces all call attention to themselves, they also serve as a perfect backdrop to the couple's artful lives.

left: *The view from
the garden shows the
powder room jutting
beyond the house's
back wall and hints at
the red epoxy coating
throughout the interior.*

right: *The kitchen
and dining areas have
views of the backyard
where Jordan designed
a shed and the patio
provides a great place
for summer dinners.*

left: *Formerly a director for Eyebeam, a Manhattan art and technology center, Melanie now works solely on her own art. The family's collection of art includes Barbara Kruger, Joan Miró, Pablo Picasso, Marc Chagall, Sylvia* *Safdie, and Giovanni Piranesi. This 18-foot mural was custom made for its unusual spot by Tali Hinkis of the digital arts group LoVid.*

right: *Melanie is an installation artist whose work incorporates video, computer graphics, and sound. Through a glass wall, her studio has a view of an Alejandro Bron sculpture located just outside the house.*

left: *Melanie's office is located in the house's basement level, which unlike most Brooklyn basements, is as airy as any other floor. Light pours into the office through a glass wall facing the garden. A pull-out couch, which is separated* *from Melanie's office by sliding glass doors, allows for guests to sleep over.*

top right: *The couple was looking to customize the house as much as possible since this is the house they hope to live in for the next several years. Here, a wall features a custom spice rack for Melanie since she loves to cook.*

bottom right: *A custom-made airplane-style bathroom carries the red color beyond the kitchen area. The bathroom straddles one of the house's voids and juts through its back wall.*

above: *Jordan kept the bedroom simple and bright, but customized the space by raising the roof at a slight angle to allow for a greater height to the space.*

previous spread:
*The free-form floor-plan allows the family to see the front, back, top, and bottom of the house from nearly any spot. However, the kitchen feels like the house's center.*

above: *Both Melanie and Jordan sometimes work at home, so their two offices were built into the house's program. Through vertical openings, the couple can see each other at opposite ends of the house.*

opposite: *The parlor floor features a marble mantel, one of the few items salvaged from the renovation. To furnish their home, Jordan and Melanie mixed pieces by local furniture designers such as Hivemindesign with well-known foreign*

*designers, such as the Bourellec brothers. A projection screen is cleverly recessed in the ceiling above the armchairs and can be lowered for watching television or movies.*

# BRENDAN
# COBURN

opposite: *Brendan Coburn has renovated dozens of brownstones in Brooklyn. With his own two-family project, Brendan kept only the front wall and gutted the interior, filling the entire space with daylight. Many of the facets in his own home were experiments later replicated for his clients.*

When Brendan Coburn talks about Brooklyn architecture, he discusses the need to applaud buildings that are "good citizens." These structures aren't designed by so-called "starchitects"; instead, these competently constructed projects enliven the cityscape without overpowering it. Brendan's work falls into this category, even if it does occasionally startle with its cleverness.

Brendan grew up in a row house in Cobble Hill with a father who practiced architecture and a mother who worked as an interior designer. "Because of its east-west orientation, it was almost always dark," Brendan says of the house. "Although I love that house, I think its darkness really affected me and made me want to look for brighter properties and pursue daylight at all costs." So when Brendan bought this Carroll Gardens residence, he was determined to let the light in.

"I think my main interest and opportunity in this house was to be much more modern in my approach to the space planning, fenestration, structure, and detailing of the project," says Brendan, who has renovated some 20 brownstones. "Neither my wife nor I was concerned about re-sale or staying within the traditional type."

What's interesting is that in his desire to defy tradition, Brendan created a template for gut renovation that he has replicated in a number of Brooklyn brownstones. Though each project calls for a unique evaluation of a building, the use of maple wood, customized cabinetry, frosted glass stairs, and stylish outdoor spaces can be found in Brendan's other residential projects around the borough.

In this particular house, only the facade was left untouched. He added a floor and also enlarged the footprint by 10 feet at the back of the house. With a tight amount of square footage and a budget that required a ground-floor tenant to pay the mortgage, the building's large glass openings keep the space light and far from feeling cramped. A glass staircase also allows light to flow in from all directions. The main floor transitions seamlessly from living room to kitchen to dining room, with cabinets cleverly concealing a refrigerator and dry foodstuffs. These astute uses of space continue upstairs where each landing doubles as a desk and bookshelves.

Are there things he would have done differently? "I would have put both bedrooms on the same floor," Brendan says, acknowledging that having his young son traipsing up and down the glass stairs isn't the most practical solution. Other than that, the family finds it just about perfect.

left: *Even in a triplex, space is at a premium. Brendan disguised much of the kitchen storage and refrigerator behind custom panels.*

right: *A brightly colored wall highlights the dining area.*

opposite: *A staircase with frosted glass landings filters light through all the levels of the center of the row house.*

next spread: *By installing large windows in the back of the house, Brendan could be certain the interior of the house would receive enough daylight. The parlor floor also has access to the backyard.*

*Gut Renovations*

above: *Even with
a relatively small floor
plate, Brendan was
able to carve out three
bedrooms, including
this one for his son.*

left: *The master suite on the top floor has a decidely softer palette of colors than the lower levels.*

right: *From the garden, one can see how Brendan extended the house 10 feet in the backyard, as well as the back wall's new facade.*

# PHILIPPE BAUMANN

*PARK SLOPE*

Unlike most gut renovations in Brooklyn, this 120-year-old brick carriage house has a definite street presence. Over the years, the building has shuffled through a variety of uses, and prior to its latest incarnation as a statement of Modern architecture, it was known for the United Airways turbine that fell through its roof in the 1960s. Most recently, when the current owners hired Phil Baumann to create a residence within its four walls, the space was being used for light industrial work.

To honor its quirky past while creating more space for a young family of five, Phil kept what materials he could and built a 1,000-square-foot second-floor addition. As a result, the main floor and stairways feature plenty of the building's vintage brick and wood, concrete, and oxidized steel. To imbue the space with an earthiness and more natural daylight, Phil coated the concrete walls with an organic limewash and punctured clerestory windows into walls on the first floor.

One of Phil's priorities was to find as many ways as possible to pull in natural light to the first floor. So when he built the upstairs loft space, he offset it by 3 feet to allow for a light well—a sort of elongated skylight—into the main living room. Such small touches strengthen the connection between indoors and out while keeping the space remarkably private.

While the first level's renovation demonstrates a deft use of material to create a space that feels far removed from the city, the second floor, which Phil calls "the best space in the house," modernizes the building both inside and out. The loft is held by 30-foot steel beams that span the existing walls. Currently, the clients' children are the primary users of that raw space—its openness is perfect for arts and crafts projects and for throwing toys around. However, with exposures in all directions, a terrace overlooking a tree-lined Park Slope street on one side, a private deck with a Jacuzzi and views of Brooklyn rooftops and beyond, this level begs to be used by adults only.

opposite: *Philippe Baumann transformed an original carriage house into a three-story home. He salvaged some of the old materials, such as old brick, while introducing new ideas and adding a striking new steel-framed second floor.*

above: *Like almost
any other narrow
structure in Brooklyn,
the house was lacking
daylight. The second
story is like a loft—
light filters in from
clerestory windows,
seen at profile here.*

*Gut Renovations*

left: *The house has unexpected indoor/ outdoor connections. As seen in other images, the colorful vegetation on and around the house filters through glass bricks and gives a warm hue to the interior.*

right: *The second story of the house features a front porch, perfect for watching pedestrians.*

*Gut Renovations*

previous spread:
*The second story loft
provides 1,000 square
feet of free space.*

left: *The bathroom
located off the loft is
as airy as an outdoor
shower.*

right: *Phil used
glass brick throughout
the house to give the
owners some privacy
and get daylight
indoors.*

*Gut Renovations*

above: *Glass brick
brings light into the
open-plan kitchen and
the rest of the first floor.*

# CHRISTIAN HUBERT

*FORT GREENE*

When talking to Brooklyn architects about the changing aesthetic of the borough, many of them refer in passing to a single, pioneering project: Christian Hubert's renovation of a brownstone and an adjacent three-story building, which he combined to create a 10,000-square-foot residence for an artist. As of completion in 2004, no other gut-renovated brownstone in Brooklyn had so boldly proclaimed its Modernism. This project changed many Brooklynites' feelings about radical transformations of centuries-old buildings and made it more acceptable for architects to pursue unusual exteriors.

When the owner bought these two buildings, they were dilapidated—typical of vacant brownstones. Having been used at various points as a Masonic temple and as an artists' studio, the buildings retained few original details that the architect or client sought to preserve. So the overhaul connected the buildings, adding a 4-foot extension from the second through fourth floors on one side and eliminating indoor space on the third floor to comply with the building code. An office occupies the garden-floor level, while the next flight up features a spacious art studio bathed in light from 10 windows. The third and fourth floors are dedicated to living and sleeping spaces. Another office perches on the fifth floor.

The owner had worked with Christian on his old residence, a loft in SoHo. "The original loft had been very inspired by 1950s modern design," Christian says, adding that he collects work by Italian designers such as Carlo Molino and Marco Zanuso. But for this project, Christian took cues from the artist's paintings and their strong contrasts of materials and images. In that vein, Christian decided to approach each building as an individual piece of a larger creation that could be unified stylistically through a common restoration. The project's color palette is muted, as if to serve as just a background for the art.

The complex dialogue between owner and architect provided another juxtaposition. "When it came to the metal addition, we had some differences in materials. I wanted to use stainless steel, but we ended up compromising with lead zinc. Each element was decided independently and we had a very active working relationship, from details such as the height of the bedroom ceiling to the choice of finishes. But we ended up with a result that we are both very happy with."

opposite: *This project inspired a number of other architects in the neighborhood to think boldly about renovating brownstones. The exterior facade combines a number of different materials: lead zinc clads the extension to the house on the east side of the house while yellow-painted concrete tiles on the ground level contrast with the body of the building's gray paint.*

above: *Designer and owner had worked together before on the owner's loft in Tribeca. Here in Brooklyn, with the luxury of combining two buildings, there was plenty of space to spread out and test new ideas about architecture and furnishings.*

above: *The kitchen is beautifully laid out. Not seen in the picture is a small breakfast nook, which completes the space and separates it from the dining area.*

next spread: *The dining area sits between kitchen (above) and living room (opposite).*

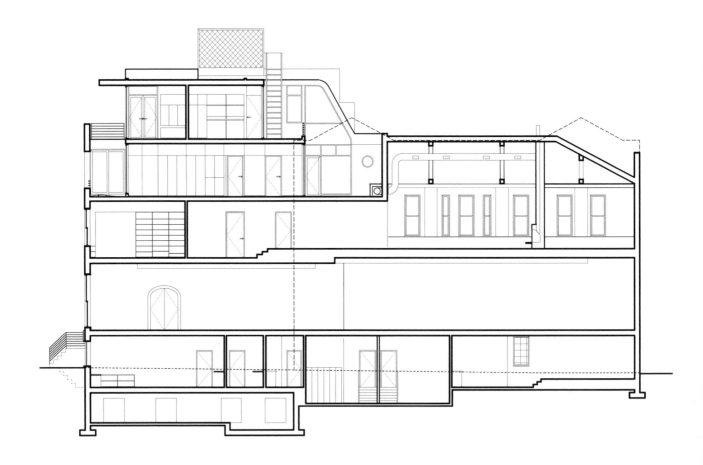

above: *The above*
*section shows how the*
*two buildings were*
*combined into one.*
*The ground floor*
*houses the owner's*
*office, the first floor*
*his studio, and the*
*next several floors*
*his living space.*
*Not registered as*

*an architect, Christian*
*collaborated with*
*Greg Merryweather*
*(page 44) on the*
*building's plans.*

left: *Unlike many single-family homes dogged by the space an internal staircase takes up, here Christian set the staircase outside the living spaces in a separate hallway.*

right: *Christian smartly hid heating elements behind this detailed wooden encasement that lines the windows on the second floor.*

above: *The master
suite features two
outdoor spaces and
reaps sunlight from
both exposures.*

above: *A certain
amount of buildable
interior space by
the city's Buildings
Department was
allotted for the
project. The idea for
these outdoor spaces
developed from
wrestling with code
requirements.*

left: *The master suite
is lit not only by
the outdoor terrace
and courtyard, but by
a clerestory window.*

right: *The master
bath features a
Japanese soaking tub
and looks out onto
the private courtyard.*

above: *The media
room features custom
cabinetry that hides all
the aesthetic problems
that come with tech-
nology. A fabric wall-
covering improves the
room's acoustics.*

# BERGEN STREET STUDIO

*BOERUM HLLL*

At some point during the past five years, Clay Miller, a founding partner of Bergen Street Studio, began noticing a new kind of Brooklyn client. "I stopped seeing so many people who were religiously devoted to detail," he says. "Looking at their brownstones' interiors, they'd say, 'There's not anything here we want to keep.' And of course that's an exciting thing for an architect to hear."

The owners of this particular Boerum Hill brownstone previously lived in a house in Midwood where they had rooms—and Victorian details—to spare. When they purchased this house, the clients consulted Clay on how to transform its several apartments into a modern triplex and a garden-level apartment for a nanny.

Clay says that his "ideal" clients, a top executive at MTV and a sound editor for such television programs as Chapelle's Show, were "quite articulate about how they wanted the space to feel as light as possible." The quest to illuminate the house, while abiding by the Landmarks Preservation Commission's regulations, meant opening spaces within the brownstone's envelope rather than opening it to the exterior. This constraint, combined with the brownstone's layout (which places a bracing wall a third of the way into each floorplate) inspired Clay to rethink the focus on living vertically.

Placing a three-story light well at the entrance of the house—a risky move—eliminates the awkward space created by the bracing wall. Light filtering from this space hits all levels through glass openings on each floor, which Clay says "adds drama to emphasize the vertical." To further dramatize the top floor, Clay had the ceiling height lifted (although there is no evidence of the alteration from the street). Clay acknowledges his clients' confidence in the process, which he says gave him the freedom to experiment.

The clients, both media professionals, felt strongly about tastefully containing their sprawl of audio-visual equipment. They also hoped to recreate the Midwood house's storage in this less forgiving floorplan. Clay found John Brennan, of the Red Hook–based Memphis Woodworking, who was able to create quality custom cabinet space without breaking the budget. The plain-sawn maple wood of the cabinetry recalls traditional built-in mahogany pieces typical of Victorian brownstones in such a way that connects the new with the old.

opposite: *This Boerum Hill house looks like any other in the historic landmarks district. However, behind the original facade is a gut-renovated two-family house with a triple-story skylight in the entrance hall.*

*Gut Renovations*

left and right: *The three-story skylight brings daylight down into all areas of the brownstone while glass walls on each level face onto the void.*

*Gut Renovations*

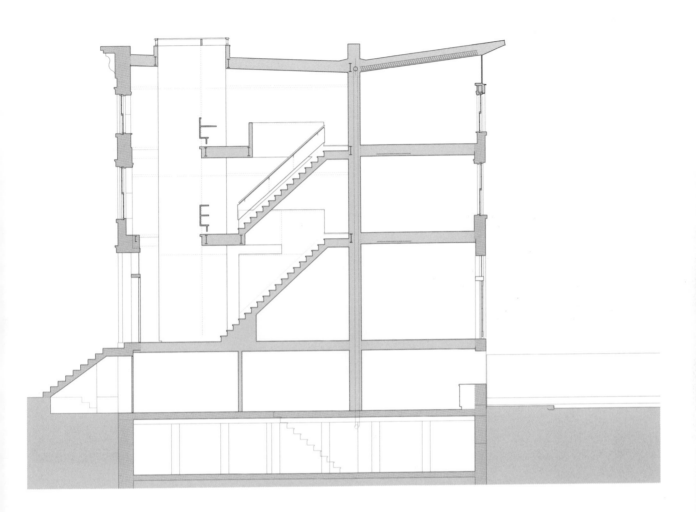

above: *A section of
the house shows how
the light well breaks
up the monotony of the
brownstone floorplan
and opens all levels
to light. Also, the roof
was raised slightly in
the back.*

above: *A big part
of the project was
devising storage for
the family's needs.
In the living room,
audio visual equip-
ment is hidden
in seamless, maple
cabinetry.*

above: *Clay used the*
*maple wood to create*
*a core that encloses*
*bathroom, bookshelves,*
*and kitchen cabinetry.*

left: *The bathroom's blue-green tiles are in keeping with the pale blues and purples that color the walls throughout the house.*

right: *Sliding doors separate the master suite from the staircase. A small office is set into a nook overlooking the light well.*

opposite: *One of the owners' daughter's bedrooms presents a view of old and new— landmarked windows butt up against blue-tinged glass and built-in desk.*

# SUSAN BOYLE & BENTON BROWN

*CROWN HEIGHTS*

It was November 2001 when Susan Boyle and Benton Brown bought a plot of six buildings in Crown Heights. The couple, who had been living near the Brooklyn Navy Yard, had been looking to buy a vacant building—and had found more than they could handle. They kept the two buildings with the most architectural integrity and sold off the neighboring ones to finance a massive renovation. Their first project: Develop one of the buildings as five rental units, with an enormous duplex on the top floor for themselves.

The first building they renovated was once known as the Nassau Brewery Ice House. The building, which had its enormous ceiling heights bisected by additional floors, was in shambles. The gut renovation was made slightly less daunting because both Susan and Benton have backgrounds in construction and planning. As a welder, Benton had some previous experience in construction and renovation. Susan's former job concerned sustainable transportation and architecture; her expertise helped her make informed choices regarding the building's sustainable elements.

The major elements of the renovation included creating four floors from seven, fixing the sinking foundation, pouring new concrete and adding new utilities. Making the process as sustainable and environment-friendly as possible provided an added challenge. But the couple, who used their other building as a storage and staging area, salvaged more than 400 wood beams. All the wood used in the project is recycled—including beams in the ceiling, wood planks on the floors, even the furniture. Because their plans for the buildings are very long term—"we have a 30-year plan," Susan says—their environmentally keen choices will pay off in spades. Rather than install air-conditioning, for instance, large windows allow for plenty of air circulation and cross ventilation. Radiant heat from the fly-ash concrete floors, Energy Star–rated appliances, and boilers and hot water thermostats installed in each apartment save energy. Lastly, many fixtures such as tubs and sinks were salvaged, and furniture is made from recycled materials.

With one building's renovation completed in 2004, they began the renovation of the other building; it will provide the community with small commercial spaces. Susan and Benton continue to consult for other Brooklynites interested in green roof installations and environmental renovations. Publicity surrounding the project has garnered the couple attention, and they've become known for their knowledge of green architecture and construction. "We try to help anyone who calls with suppliers and ideas," says Susan, who acknowledges that while challenging and risky, the rewards of green projects are infinitely greater than those reaped by standard renovations.

*Gut Renovations*

left and right: *The couple's top priority for this project was to make it as environmentally sustainable as possible. The view from the backyard shows how even rainwater is collected from the gutters. On top of the shed lies yet another green roof. Inside, almost all the furnishings are vintage.*

above: *Before renovation, the previous owners had stuffed extra levels into each floor. Susan and Benton restored the building to double-height stories. The living areas of the duplex are open plan. The floors* *are fly-ash concrete with radiant heat.*

*Gut Renovations*

*Susan Boyle & Benton Brown*

previous spread: *Hundreds of wooden beams were salvaged from the renovation and repurposed. Here, they constructed a bookcase, which cleverly serves as a room divider as well.*

above and right: *The apartment also serves as the couple's office.*

left: *As the couple added an extra floor to the building, they also added a green roof, which was still in bloom by late fall.*

right: *Luckily, the view from Crown Heights is still panoramic from a few stories up.*

left and right: *The light-filled master bath features repurposed wooden beams and vintage fixtures.*

above: *The bedroom features closets made from old ambulance doors.*

next spread: *A look at the kitchen from the grand staircase that leads to the upstairs bedrooms. The kitchen island, cabinets, and shelves were made from salvaged wood.*

*Gut Renovations*

*Susan Boyle & Benton Brown*

# MICHAEL MCGINN
# & SHARON GRESH

*CARROLL GARDENS*

Originally constructed in 1961 as a garage, this two-story building was renovated into an ideal live/work space by Michael McGinn and his wife and business partner, Sharon Gresh. Using their own instincts as graphic designers and brand specialists, Michael and Sharon designed the renovation and then collaborated with friends and colleagues, Gabriel Crettol and Len Mayer of Crettol Mayer Design, to execute the construction.

The garage was built after the original owner tore down two row houses and filled the resulting double lot to the fullest extent; the building was then divided into a voluminous downstairs space where large trucks were housed and an upstairs apartment/office. In renovating the two 2,100-square-foot (30' x 70') floors, the couple kept the design simple—painted all the walls white, kept the concrete floors, installed an enormous frosted-glass garage door, made storage and modular tables out of plywood and metal, and hung some pendulum lights. It sounds somewhat simple, but complexity can be found in the details.

For example, he ground floor was set on a slope so that when the trucks were washed down, water would flow into a drain. This circumstance required that the shelving and tables be customized to accommodate the slanted floors. ("The shortest person sits at the end of the table where it's the lowest,"Michael jokes.)

Upstairs, modern furniture and plenty of storage complete a sleek space. Skylights are carved out of every room. It looks like a conscientious attempt to bring daylight into the apartment, but in fact, the openings were inserted to comply with local building code. Although unlikely, new construction nearby could block the bedroom windows, and skylights had to be created to accommodate the humane need for fresh air and light.

Michael and Sharon were open to experimentation: walls lined with maple veneered plywood panels and a kitchen made from medical appliance cabinetry show the couple's enthusiasm for personalized solutions to everyday needs.

opposite: *Michael McGinn and Sharon Gresh run a design firm that specializes in brand identity. They found this former garage years ago and slowly designed its conversion into a live/ work duplex.*

left: *The main living area sits right beneath a huge skylight. Michael and Sharon had originally envisioned building above this space, but building code didn't allow for the addition.*

right: *To maximize the space, the bedrooms are aligned, railroad-style, along a main corridor. Another living area is placed at the end of it.*

above: *The open
kitchen is made from
cabinets usually used
in doctors' offices.*

*Gut Renovations*

opposite, left, and right: *The main floor of the duplex is a voluminous office space. Partly out of necessity and partly out of creativity, the shelving and tables were all made by Michael using stock materials.*

*Michael's designs better accomodate the sloping floor.*

*Otherwise, the space was kept to its bare bones—concrete blocks are left unpainted and unadorned lights hang from the ceiling.*

above: *A small room*
*affords space for a den/*
*office at the back end*
*of the apartment.*

*Gut Renovations*

above: *All of the
bedrooms feature sky-
lights, but not for
obvious reasons:
Building code requires
access to fresh air
should the windows
on the walls be covered
if a new building were
to block them.*

this page and
opposite: *The
den/office and master
bedroom feature mid-
century furnishings.*

# THE ROMANCE OF RENOVATION

*BY JONATHAN BUTLER*

When my wife and I walked into an open house for a circa 1860 brownstone in Clinton Hill, it was love at first sight. Or second. The night before, scrutinizing photos on the Corcoran Web site, I had proclaimed, in a moment of gallantry colored by red wine, "I'm going to buy you that house!" And so, with little more than heady romanticism to steer our course, we put in a bid for the five-story Victorian and made the first step toward a life-changing renovation.

Although our brownstone, which for many years had been used as an SRO, had retained many of its original details, we needed to upgrade it to the 21st century with all new plumbing, air-conditioning, and electrical wiring. Our previous renovation experience was limited to a one-bedroom Manhattan apartment—incomparable in terms of the historic value of the property or the scale of the project. Though mere novices, we were undaunted. Not even the asking price, a huge stretch, or the additional costs of renovation could dissuade us. Blind faith and desire won out over financial concerns.

We weren't alone in our idealism. Our Clinton Hill neighborhood—like Bedford-Stuyvesant, Fort Greene, and others—was in the midst of a renaissance. Many other young families were buying similarly beautiful brick and brownstone townhouses with dreams of making them their own—practicality be damned.

By instinct we decided to share our renovation with the community. We also wanted to keep a record of the process for ourselves. So we documented the renovation on Brownstoner, our blog about Brooklyn real estate and renovation, which we had launched a few months before buying the house. In the nine months it took to swap shag carpeting for parquet floors and linoleum for salvaged wood flooring, we learned a number of things: Several applications of paint can preserve a marble mantelpiece; in places, the party wall between adjacent brownstones is only one brick thick. We also made lots of mistakes, not least picking the contractor who made the lowest bid. But we were in good company—as evinced by the bounty of war stories, and occasional successes, posted to the Brownstoner blog.

In time, hundreds (and eventually thousands) of homeowners, renovators, and those who aspired to be one, the other, or both joined the Brownstoner community. One of the fascinating things the Web site has showed us is that, despite a generally shared respect for older architecture, there is a wide range of preferred approaches to renovating an old house. For some, a renovation means performing a perfect period restoration; others will transform the house into a piece of eco-friendly or green architecture; still others pour concrete where parquet once lay.

For our own renovation, we sought to strike a balance between our Modernist inclinations and our love of the house's original details. As a result, we restored the original architectural elements to the extent we could afford and reserved contemporary flourishes for furniture, art, and appliances.

*Gut Renovations*

Because we hewed fairly closely to preservationist standards of renovation, we are sometimes pegged as traditionalists. Not so. We love good modern design. It's just that we abhor mediocrity and lack of vision. Precisely for this reason, it is refreshing to have a reminder that in fact there are many examples of interesting, new approaches to renovating Brooklyn houses that were built for inhabitants with very different lifestyles and needs from our own. These old homes are themselves evolving organisms whose pasts need to be respected but not necessarily recreated. Many examples in this book—from the convincing renovation of two buildings into one artist's home and studio (page 110) to Noroof Architects' renovation (page 76) of a standard-looking vinyl-sided residence into a much more daring two-family home—demonstrate the vitality of architectural creativity in Brooklyn.

Although brownstone renovations have important consequences for the borough, they are only one aspect of the changing Brooklyn witnessed by residents on a daily basis. Since we launched Brownstoner.com, commentary on the site has reflected a growing concern that the booming real estate market is leaving its mark in negative ways. Developers with no interest in the future of a neighborhood have squeezed construction onto every last square foot of space across the borough; high profile architects have been caught signing off on plans that do not conform to code; the safety of site workers has been neglected as contractors pursue ever-greater profits. What is most frustrating about these abuses, which have a much greater effect on the public than the modification of brownstone interiors, is how diametrically opposed they are to the values of community and respect for the past that so many Brooklynites hold close to their hearts.

In light of discussions on Brownstoner regarding undesirable development across the borough, we point out that inexpensive design is not necessarily ugly or thoughtless. We exhort developers to think "bigger," to embrace creative solutions, and to realize that small, incremental improvements can translate into an end-product that is more pleasing to the community and also more profitable. Indeed, much of the work in the book is proof of that.

Long before the term "luxury condo" entered the vernacular, Brooklyn inspired a kind of stoop culture engendered by people who cared about the fabric of the community— something Brownstoner has tried to recreate online as stoops have given way to lobbies and tall buildings.

The economics of real estate in Brooklyn have changed, and the architectural reference points have, too. But residents, homeowners, architects, and developers shouldn't disregard the culture so long cultivated in our neighborhoods. Brooklyn thrives on its diversity of backgrounds, opinions, and styles. But what truly distinguishes it from Manhattan, say, is the resourcefulness apparent in those who, like us, scrape together a down payment on a house that's bigger and more beautiful than they ever imagined possible in New York City.

# NEW WORK

—

*PART THREE*

*THE MOST EXCITING EXPRESSION OF BROOKLYN'S ARCHITECTURAL VITALITY IS THE WORK THAT IS BUILT FROM THE GROUND UP. THESE HOUSES, WHICH REFLECT THE VERNACULAR OF THE BROWNSTONE, OFTEN SEEM INFLUENCED BY STYLES FOUND ELSEWHERE— LOS ANGELES OR SAN FRANCISCO OR LONDON. MOST INTERESTING TO ME IS THAT THEIR BOLD FACADES CALL ATTENTION TO THEMSELVES, YET PROFESS MODESTY THROUGH THEIR MATERIALS AND BUDGET. SADLY, THE DAYS OF THE CHEAP VACANT LOT SEEM TO BE OVER IN BROOKLYN, AND PERHAPS, GOING FORWARD, FEWER NEW PROJECTS SUCH AS THESE WILL BE BUILT.*

# DAVID
# ADJAYE

*CLINTON HILL*

As this townhouse was under construction, mystery shrouded it much like its unique black facade. Who designed it? Was this a person's home, and if so, whose? And what was that facade made from? That David Adjaye, a renowned young architect based in London, was revealed to be behind all the fuss made perfect sense. David, who often works with a dark and experimental palette, has earned a loyal following in the art world for his houses and museums. Who else could so masterfully design studios for two artists (who happened to be friends of his) already living in the neighborhood?

Located adjacent to a church parking lot, this townhouse's parcel originally contained a small garage, torn down to accommodate the four-story building. Built from the ground up, the structure includes two studios and two offices stacked on top of each other. But not stacked like the pancake floorplans in traditional brownstones. Instead, the studios are dramatic, soaring spaces that both have outdoor access, via a triple-story curtainwall. Through that first-floor studio, double doors open to a concrete garden space. This space is very much the opposite of a typical Brooklyn back yard—it exalts in that most urban of materials: concrete. The concrete frames pine and myrtle trees, planted in witty circular cutouts, and also forms a long, rectangular fountain.

From the first-floor studio, one can ascend a central staircase to the other levels or take the hidden stair between the second and third floors. David enlivened what could have been standard byways with concrete handrails lit by fluorescent bulbs, which set up the play of positive and negative space carried throughout the house.

The second floor features an office and another double-height studio space that overlooks the garden. This studio is capped by a pyramid roof. Strategically placed skylights add to the abundance of natural light. An exposed staircase leads to another office on the third floor.

Though the complex approach to structure intrigues, smaller moments demonstrate a nuanced response to typical townhouse details. The mysterious facade is made of woven plastic panels that contrast with neighboring earthen materials like brick and brownstone. The interior flaunts white walls and black-stained wooden floors, with the gray poured-concrete kitchen and customized timber bookshelves providing the only hints of color. Working with architect of record David Hotson, an architect whose excellent work can be found in another single-family home in Williamsburg, both Davids show the possibilities for innovation when one is not afraid to shock or stand out.

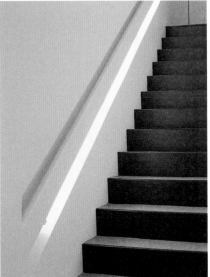

left: *David is known for his enigmatic, dark exteriors and minimalist interiors.*

right and opposite left: *What could have been boring, standardized staircases are reinvented as dramatic spaces with concrete handrails and their negative spaces, all made of one piece, and lit by fluorescent bulbs.*

right: *Small vig-*
*nettes such as this*
*step down window*
*seat and observation*
*area explore the*
*different planes of*
*space throughout the*
*building. Standing*
*there, one can look*
*up into an internal*
*void that reaches*

*the ceiling or out to*
*the street.*

opposite: *The third floor studio receives light from strategically placed skylights, windows, and a Dutch door which opens to the back yard below. Ebonized wood floors work to dramatic effect as the only dark element in the house's* *design. Here, the same wood used for all the custom cabinetry forms built-in furniture and a staircase leading to the fourth-floor office.* above: *Mia, one of the office assistants, sits in the top-floor office.*

left: *The first floor's poured-in-place concrete kitchen.*

right: *A view of the first-floor studio from the second floor. The studio's double doors lead to the backyard.*

*New Work*

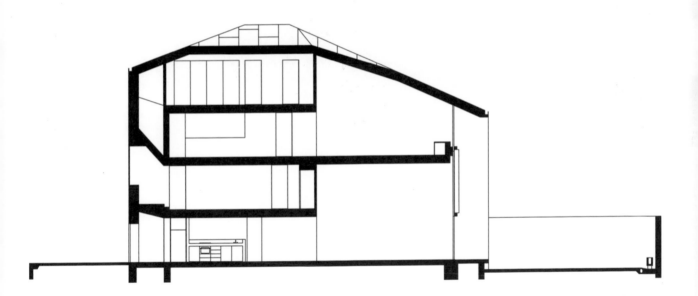

above: *A section of
the townhouse demon-
strates just how
unusual its layout
and profile are.*

top left: *Even a simple
shower stall in the
upstairs bathroom is
bathed in sunlight and
adheres to David's high
aesthetic standards.*

top right: *The wood
staircases leading
up to the top-floor office
have small notches
that provide a small
decorative effect
for an otherwise spare
construction.*

left: *The second-floor office features custom-made built-in cabinetry with high shelf heights that can accommodate the artist's collection of monographs and other oversized art books.*

right: *Unlike most Brooklyn back yards, this one is paved over with concrete. Pine and myrtle trees grow through circular cut-outs. A poured-concrete fountain sits in the back.*

opposite: *Glass panels form the back wall of the townhouse and give more reflections of the neighboring brownstones than insight into the interior.*

David Adjaye

# TINA MANIS

*BOERUM HILL*

When Tina Manis was commissioned to build a townhouse on a vacant lot located half a block from housing projects, she was surprised to find that the clients (a young couple with a toddler) wanted elements suited to a house in a more rural location: grass, a garage, privacy, and plenty of light. What she came up with is the perfect solution for the owners—a three-bedroom duplex with landscaped backyard and a rental unit on the third floor with a roofdeck.

Tina managed to achieve her client's goals while imbuing the project with something of the sunny disposition that characterizes new architecture in her native California. The front of the townhouse is covered with wood slats placed in a variegated pattern. It's a type of facade that challenges the brownstone status quo and calls into question the borough's love of ornament—it feels politely subversive. The texture of the slats echoes the unevenness of brownstones protruding in and out of their lots, and of buckling bluestone sidewalks. The slats also work well to disguise a garage door and entrance to the rental unit, giving the impression of a rather large single-family home. Tina cleverly set back the third floor to provide all tenants a sense of privacy from every direction.

In the duplex, budgetary constraints kept the architectural interventions rather simple. A standard floorplan is enlivened by sliding pocket doors, brightly colored furniture, and natural light. Many of the details are fashioned from inexpensive materials, such as penny tile in the bathrooms. Most walls were painted a very light blue, which looks white, but compliments the dark-blue stain on the floors.

The architecture creates great dramatic effect indoors by profiting from its interaction with the outdoors. The master bedroom features enormous windows and a balcony overlooking the back yard, while the main living space downstairs is separated from the garden by just a glass wall. Appearing to prize privacy from the front, the house revels in its openness from the back yard.

opposite: *On a vacant lot in Boerum Hill, Tina Manis designed a two-family home that has many more amenities than an older house could provide. Sleekly hidden into the wood facade is a garage door, an entrance to the main duplex, and an entrance for a rental unit on the top floor. The wooden panels, placed in an irregular pattern, emulate the slightly uneven pattern of brownstones on the block or even buckling sidewalks.*

left and right: *The
backyard is accessible
from the main living
space and can be seen
from the entryway.
A staircase with bright
orange banisters
leads upstairs to the
bedrooms.*

above: *The glass curtainwall separating the interior from the backyard contrasts with the private front facade. A deep blue stain was applied to the floors.*

next spread: *With the curtains entirely open, the master bedroom has a view of brownstones and backyards. A slight uptick in the ceiling by the window gives the feeling of a limitless ceiling height.*

above: *The open
kitchen has a lovely
view toward the
backyard; laundry
and service areas
are hidden behind it.
Whenever possible,
Tina uses energy-
efficient appliances and
sustainable materials.*

left: *Offices for husband and wife line the bedroom wall.*

right: *Tina looked for ways to maximize effect with minimal cash. Contrasting shades of penny tile brighten a bathroom without much expense.*

above: *A sliding door in the bedroom creates privacy for the room and when opened reveals bright green paint.*

opposite: *The view of the townhouse from the backyard shows all three levels of the house, as well as the roof deck.*

# BILL
# HARVEY

If you talk to designer Bill Harvey and his wife, historian Jeanne Houck, they will wax rhapsodic about Williamsburg—the good old days before the condo craze when they were the young kids hanging out on the street. But they also describe it as a place where dreams for a new architecture could be realized— a much more recent past.

With that idealism in mind, Bill says, their house shows that "you can build a new domestic architecture that doesn't have to cost 10 trillion dollars." The house, which functions well as a refuge for the family of four, is also an experiment in living.

Bill and Jeanne moved to Greenpoint in 1985 and since then Bill has become a part of the Brooklyn style scene—he renovated the 3rd Ward studio and workspace and designed a number of Brooklyn Industries stores. In 1998, the couple bought a one-story garage in Williamsburg—it took about seven years to design and construct additional floors before the place was habitable.

Their program called for keeping the garage and digging a basement to pour a new slab that would reinforce the structure. Columns placed every 12 feet support the upper floors. "I've always been involved in architecture and approached it like sculpture," says Bill, a trained sculptor and designer.

How is the layout structured? "The first floor is about the street, the second floor is about family, and the third floor is about the sky," Bill says. And indeed, the garage door on the first floor opens to allow for a huge entrance onto the street. It's where the family throws parties and sometimes allows film crews to shoot music videos or movies. The second floor is where the family lives—the kitchen and the living areas flow together as if in a loft, and a balcony looks out to the Empire State Building or to passersby below. The third floor features four bedrooms decorated with vibrant colors and vintage furniture.

Throughout the house, there was a conscientious initiative to use recycled materials—old sinks and tiles and plastics that Bill salvaged. "Aesthetically, I wanted to create a space that incorporates the energy of the street, but that's also private. The design program needed to be simple and affordable to build. It had to be elegant but also a place for the kids' energy and to give them space to spread out."

opposite: *Bill Harvey and Jeanne Houck saw potential in a one-story garage and bought it, planning to build on top of it. Bill kept the garage largely unfinished and uses it as a studio and multipurpose space. The two stories above house his family in sleek, loftlike spaces.*

left, right, and next
spread: *Unlike many
designers, Bill wasn't
afraid of using dark
and bold colors in his
house. The floors are
stained dark brown,
while black accents are
found throughout the
house. To enliven the
spaces, bright colors*
*are used liberally on the
third floor.*

above: *The open
kitchen connects to the
dining area (opposite
page) and looks out
onto a backyard patio
atop the original
garage roof.*

*New Work*

left: *Many of the
materials used in the
house were salavaged
from estate sales
or even department
stores closing down.
For example, even the
tiles for the bathroom
(above; part of the
master suite) are not
brand new. Using*
*older materials not
only saves money but
is desirably sustainable.*

above and opposite:
*The kids' bedrooms*
*emulate the vintage*
*style and bold colors*
*found throughout the*
*rest of the house.*

next spread: *The*
*master bedroom is*
*a serene space with*
*views out to McCarren*
*Park and Manhattan.*

above: *The main
living area is equal
parts the domain
of adults and kids.*

right: *A chair in
the master bedroom.*

left: *The door leading to the master bedroom features a salvaged plastic material that Bill, a products designer, has been experimenting with.*

right: *Bill and Jeanne stand in the studio.*

# ROGERS MARVEL

opposite: *Rogers Marvel won a competition to design the 14 State Street townhouses that are the first part of a master plan to develop a square block of Downtown Brooklyn. Developed by Hamlin Ventures and Time Equities, the townhouses have two main floor plans and sizes. When we photographed the showhouse, it still had a collection of artworks and furniture designs that were part of an exhibition called* Blockparty.

When they placed the winning bid on a block of Brooklyn in late 2001, Abby Hamlin and Francis Greenberger earned the enviable chance to design a swath of the city. They hired top architects who could bridge the traditional, centuries-old buildings of Boerum Hill with the jumble of styles in downtown Brooklyn. In doing so, these developers took the opportunity to start a conversation about how we define neighborhoods, architecture, and modernism.

With a variety of code regulations to abide by, Abby first got to work on the plot dedicated to a baker's dozen of brownstone-size buildings. She invited four local firms to compete to create a design that reimagines the brownstone typology. "Rogers Marvel came up with a brilliant analysis," Abby says, adding that it was ultimately that firm's thinking process that won her over. Rogers Marvel's plan reflected research and a special consideration of corner brownstones, enabling the architects to fit an additional unit which the other firms had not suggested.

The row consists of two formal types of townhouses with variations in color and material. "I was very concerned with composition and didn't want the block to feel flat, monolithic. I wanted to see how we could explore modernism in a historic setting," Abby says. To achieve that goal, the facades of the 14 townhouses recreate some of the natural rhythms found on the streets of Brooklyn, where Italianate brownstones butt against Greek Revival ones and frame houses.

"The other factor that I was concerned about was natural light," says Abby. "I didn't want these houses to feel dark like some townhouses feel." In each house, a glass curtainwall opens the back of the house to tremendous natural light, while an open floor plan doesn't obstruct the flow of 4,000 square feet (give or take a few hundred square feet depending on the model). So much space could feel cold with stark, white walls, but oak wood floors warm the space and the exposed staircase hints at movement.

"I also knew I wanted drama!" Abby says. A glass balcony overlooks the dining area and, beyond it, the backyard, which ties the public spaces together while adding excitement to the whole composition.

With each development project, Abby makes an effort to engage the public. For this venture, she collaborated with Karen Auster of Auster Events to develop *Blockparty*—an exhibition of work by some 42 designers and 25 artists, all of whom live in Brooklyn. The townhouses, together with *Blockparty*, which attracted thousands of visitors, demonstrate the extent to which Brooklyn modernism is still evolving.

above: *Ethan Ames
designed a sculptural
bench for the private
backyard.*

left and right: *An installation by Erwin Redl lines the entryway to the garden floor. The bench in the garden floor mud room was made by Brooklyn Royal and is called* Dedication No. 1.

next spread: *The kitchen faces out to the backyard. The barstools were handcrafted by Palo Samko.*

*New Work*

above: *The main
living space is as airy
as a loft and overlooks
the downstairs dining
area and backyard.
Abby specified that the
internal staircase not
clutter the interior.*

above: *From the
windows in the living
area, one can look
out at State Street.
The Italianate and
Greek Revival
buildings across the
street influenced
the composition of the
townhouses.*

left: *The staircase leading from the roof downstairs channels daylight from the skylight.*

right: *One of the bedrooms upstairs.*

left: *The living room looks onto the dining area and gives some drama to the space. The Bubble Chandeliers are by Lindsey Adelman.*

right: *The master bedroom. The project was a participant in the NYSERDA program (New York State Energy and Research and Development Authority). The building performance and key mechanical* *systems exceed all required efficiencies by 30%.*

# CHRISTOFF
# FINIO

*FORT GREENE*

opposite: *Built on a vacant lot, this house blends into the neighborhood with its subtly modern facade. The home of an artist, a musician, and their two young children, the building's four floors include studios and living spaces.*

Darcy Miro and Lars Weiss had lived in Fort Greene for several years before they noticed a vacant lot while walking their dogs to a nearby park. The space presented an opportunity to commission a 21st-century brownstone. But because the lot is only one block outside Fort Greene's historic district, the project called for a conscientious approach to the local vernacular.

There were a number of reasons why the two wanted to build anew rather than renovate. "We looked at different houses in the neighborhood, whole farmhouses with porches and old brownstone buildings. But they were inhabited or SROs," Darcy says. "We weren't going to kick someone out. The realtors were so nonchalant, 'You just have two families you have to evict.' How could we do that to a family?"

The two walls that existed on either side of the lot provided another attraction; they now form the interior walls of the brownstone. Darcy and Lars agreed to keep a relatively skeletal floor plan, with only a few planes suspended between these two walls.

The couple commissioned Christoff Finio, in part because Darcy had worked with Martin Finio on the Folk Art Museum in Manhattan. "We needed someone who was willing to take on more hours than they were going to get paid for," Darcy says "Someone who would work together with us and have it be a collaboration." Because the Christoff Finio practice had opened only recently, the firm was willing to take on an exciting project with a small budget. Marvelling at the placement of windows in the house, she says, "They made a perfect combination of home and architecture."

The brownstone quietly asserts itself as modern, without disrupting the rhythm of the street. Windows placed asymmetrically along the facade don't compete with a brick facade that echoes neighboring multifamily brick buildings.

The architects used the two existing walls—one brick, one concrete—on either side of the lot to serve as boundaries and material motifs in the creation of the family home. These two walls, along with the space's poured concrete floors, exposed pipes, steel railings, and high ceilings, the rooms feel industrial—like a renovated space, rather than a new one. But cedar beams, bright-colored furniture, and art (a portfolio from the Brooklyn Academy of Music and pieces made by friends) give the house a cozy feel.

"The space has a lot of emotional value. I touched every single part of the house while we worked on it," says Darcy. She adds, "Martin truly wanted us to have a place that we could enjoy, and which family and friends could enjoy, too. You feel that."

202

*New Work*

left and right: *It was
important to Darcy
and Lars that the
exterior facade provide
enough privacy while
still allowing for
daylight. Asymetrical
slits of windows solved
that problem.*

*New Work*

above: *The kitchen
bridges dining and
living spaces.*

above: *Darcy's studio
is filled with the colors
and creativity seen
throughout the rest
of the house. While
working on a project for
the Folk Art Museum,
she met architect
Martin Finio who
designed the house.*

left: *Darcy's studio accesses the garden and backyard patio.*

right: *The staircase leading from the first floor studios to the ground floor.*

next spread: *A view of the living area from the mezzanine level shows Lars and Darcy's eclectic taste for mid-century and contemporary furniture.*

left: *The dining area is located just off the kitchen. Many of the pieces of art found throughout the house were wedding presents to the couple and purchased at the Brooklyn Academy of Music, just a few blocks away.*

right: *Darcy loved the existing brick wall that the lot shared with a neighboring building. Wooden plank flooring adds to the rusticity of the space.*

above: *The mezzanine
was initially intended
as a den/library but
was quickly converted
into a playroom for the
kids. Metal railings
and exposed beams
add to the industrial
look of the space.*

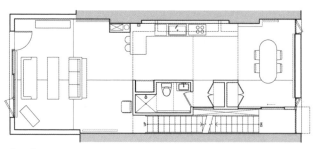

first floor

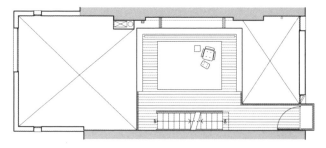

mezzanine

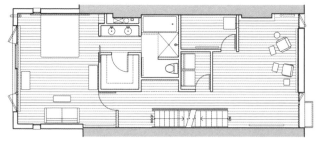

second floor

left: *The family stands on their rooftop, which has views over to Fort Greene Park and Downtown Brooklyn.*

right: *The floor plan depicts the skeletal composition of the townhouse.*

opposite: *The main living space accesses the backyard.*

# SHELTER ME

*BY ROBERT IVY*

Brooklyn shelters you. If hyper-dense Manhattan offers more zip to the inch, its streets can prove relentless. Cross the East River, however, on the magisterial Brooklyn Bridge, Our Bridge, and the pace calms in these low-rise neighborhoods that spread 71 square miles across the tip of Long Island. Its 2.5 million people return each evening to this maternal place, a city in its own right (still the would-be fourth-largest in the United States) that glorifies urban homes and urban neighborhoods.

Not a day passes in New York when I emerge from the subway or the occasional taxi without a sense of exhilaration: The neighborhood's urban richness and beauty continually surprise me. Those feelings have remained constant for almost 11 years. As with many other new arrivals, my quest for a house in New York began in Manhattan, near my midtown office, but quickly moved east as costs and dissatisfaction escalated with each real estate encounter. Who could imagine an eight-foot-wide apartment?

On a sunny Memorial Day weekend, breezy-bright, as my wife (a Park Slope native) and I toured the borough, we stopped at the foot of Montague Street in Brooklyn Heights. Outdoor cafes bustled with locals drinking coffee, reading the *Times,* and soaking up the sun; moms and dads chatted with friends while pushing strollers; flags and banners whipped lightly on storefronts. Down at the Promenade, Manhattan's towers glinted over the water—close but separate. I knew at that moment the car need go no further: We were home. That W.H. Auden had lived around the corner, as had Truman Capote, and that Lewis Mumford had once lived next door only added to this writer's sense of arrival.

A walk through neighboring streets today brings a similar realization. The densely settled houses rise four or five stories, punctuated by the occasional unexpected Spanish revival apartment hotel from the 1920s. Styles vary dramatically from iconic stoop-fronted brownstone facades to historic revivals. Materials range from brownstone to brick to clapboard. Some sport rich ornamentation in carved stone with welcoming arms constructed of curved ironwork, while others retain a Greek Revival austerity. All sit cheek by jowl, united by sidewalks made of flagstone pavers, and streets of London Plane trees or maples or the occasional gingkgoes that sometimes touch. Tiny gardens insert a speck of green by the elevated doorways, or in spring, gold forsythia. The harmonic unity of the streetscape seems textured, immeasurably rich with a language that can be read like a musical score. If the language seems overly optimistic, credit it to a spring morning.

Part of the continual fascination with the place lies in the past, in the blend of history and myth rooted there, from the 17th-century Dutch farmsteads and Revolutionary sites to Jackie Robinson and the Dodgers; egg creams and cheesecake and Nathan's original hot dog; and people like my neighbor, a 10th-generation New Yorker now in her nineties with a recognizable Dutch name who sits by our stoop on sunny days, greets little dogs out for a stroll with their human partners, and in a stentorian voice warns off anyone silly enough to nudge a car onto the sidewalk. Otis Pratt Pearsall, who with his wife Nancy helped inaugurate New York's first historic district in November 1965, still keeps a vigilant watch nearby. Shades of Henry Ward Beecher and the Underground Railroad, Walt Whitman, architect Richard Upjohn, Shirley Chisholm, Hart Crane, and Marilyn Monroe hover around the place.

Part of the borough's attraction lies in the coolness/hipness that is engendered by a new generation, many of whom could care less about the past, a group that is moving across the river in droves, populating Williamsburg and Greenpoint and Red Hook and lower Park Slope, and turning Smith Street in Carroll Gardens and Fourth Avenue and Gowanus and parts of Fort Greene into an outer Village, (as in Greenwich). And contemporary writers seemingly populate every block, from Jumpa Lahiri and Paul Auster to Ron Chernow and Jonathan Lethem. Everyone loves to ride a wave on the ascent.

New and old are drawn to the scale, which illustrates Jane Jacobs's urban principles, now practically a religion: three-dimensionally (low-rise, high density pushed to their outer limits) and the felicitous mix of uses found there, where businesses often take the garden or the first floors, residences the upper ones. They are also lured by rentals and condo developments that are sprouting up reeking of contemporized authenticity. Take the 14 State Street townhouses development near downtown Brooklyn, in which a Manhattanite constructed houses at a competitive cost, designed by the well-known architectural firm Rogers Marvel. These buildings coexist beautifully with their older neighbors across the street, yet offer a contemporary interpretation of townhouse living. A model house featured original artwork by a new generation of Brooklyn artists and craftspeople.

Yet the physical Brooklyn I have been describing, without the influx, would be largely familiar to Fort Greene native Marianne Moore, for the first, great neighborhoods only brush the tip of the rounded island. Major arterials go deep, cross or circle the end of Long Island, giving definition to Brooklyn: from its urban core just off the Brooklyn Bridge, out through the borough on Flatbush or Eastern Parkway (an early Olmstead plan) or Atlantic Avenue. These arteries ribbon the perimeter, broadly cutting past Borough Hall to the great art moderne library at Grand Army Plaza and the Botanic Garden and the Brooklyn Museum, before ultimately finding their way to the sea.

Much of the borough is renewing itself. According to New York's Department of City Planning, change is coming to seminal, wide Flatbush Avenue, which that department is working to improve for pedestrians, and to the burgeoning arts district near the Brooklyn Academy of Music, which will eventually contain a library for theater and the arts by Enrique Norten, housing, and more. Some neighborhoods seem to ache for creative investment, such as Coney Island, where we can easily imagine a major entertainment precinct attracting international visitors. Others, like Bay Ridge or Bensonhurst, remain happily grounded, in no real danger of altering their stability.

Back to the river. After a decade of debate, the Department of City Planning, under commissioner Amanda Burden, has been working to change zoning laws along 180 blocks at the riverfront, encouraging much-needed mixed-use and residential development in formerly industrial zones, while limiting property heights of new buildings to six stories near the waterfront. To spur a more equitable mix of housing types, the addition of affordable units to new market-rate housing results in valuable development rights. As a direct result of regulatory changes, Williamsburg and Greenpoint are already witnessing the punctuation of the skyline with new vertical residences.

Throughout the borough, neighborhoods with familiar names each have a story to tell. At Red Hook, cruise ships began to call at the docks, in an expansion of maritime and industrial development. DUMBO, the shadowy warehouse precinct between the Brooklyn and Manhattan bridges, has shifted from industrial to arts to yuppie housing and now welcomes them all to Art at St. Ann's, where Roseanne Cash sang on a recent evening, and the chocolate store purveyed its hand-made delicacy to the perambulating crowds. Just outside, the State of New York is in the process of realizing the expansion of Fulton Ferry State Park and Brooklyn Bridge Park, which will extend recreational areas along the waterfront for 1.5 miles of former dockland and industrial land at the foot of the promenade, up to DUMBO at the Manhattan Bridge.

Park Slope, where my wife's old house still stands on Third Street, has slipped farther and farther down the hill. No longer cut off at Seventh Avenue (a longtime scene), the action has moved to Fifth as a restaurant street, and even lower. Litanies have been written (and movies made) over the Slope's easy living (some call it the Berkeley of the East Coast), with running or walking and socializing and sleeping and all kinds of couples and African drumming in Prospect Park. But parking throughout the Slope has turned into a nightmare, a daily battle for a nonexistent spot on the residential streets. As a witness to the area's desirability, the architect Richard Meier designed the first major contemporary high-rise condominium building in Prospect Heights overlooking Grand Army Plaza, set to open in 2007. Manhattan high style is arriving, but are we ready?

What of the hard-bitten neighborhoods? Bushwick, site of riots during the 1977 blackout, is morphing into trendoid "East Williamsburg" as lower crime rates and an influx of affluent residents transform its demographics. In Brownsville, the city is investing in affordable housing. Overall in low-income neighborhoods, the level of disinvestment (read: abandonment by landlords) that had plagued the poorest areas during the 1960s and 1970s has shifted course—not completely, but the process does seem to be waning. Still, some neighborhoods like East New York await the magic kiss of 21st-century affluence.

As in any vibrant international center, different populations inhabit buildings originally intended for others. Today, whites are moving into Bed-Stuy, with its trove of brownstones and history of diversity; Caribbeans have taken hold in Carnasie; South Asians and Russians inhabit Midwood. Brighton Beach has borne the moniker "Little Odessa" for years. The borough's fabled accent may have dissipated (who remembers the receptionists or salespeople who called you *deah*?), but our language has been enriched by Mandarin and Jamaican lilts.

A cacophony of complaints have centered on a recent development. No project in recent memory has provoked more furor or sent more vocal adherents to the barricades than the 22-acre Atlantic Yards project. This mega-development by the Forest City Ratner Company will feature a major sports arena for the Nets basketball franchise (which ostensibly has strong support), together with 16 mixed-use buildings, including a hotel, office space, retail, and approximately 6,400 housing units—all in a single planned development near the confluence of Atlantic and Flatbush Avenues. From my late adolescence until today, the neighborhood has been struck with a kind of crummy emptiness brought about by the Long Island Railroad train yard. We all agree that something needed to be done.

But at this scale? Dissension has come over the necessity of closing off certain streets, in the sheer numbers of people—residents and workers—that will be loosed on the borough's challenged infrastructure (so many cars, so little parking), and the physical affect on the gentrifying neighborhoods surrounding the development. Furthermore, a single architect, Frank Gehry, has been commissioned to design all major structures, rendering the totality with an expressionist style that marks the moment of its making. Gehry, while undeniably great, will have "branded" central Brooklyn—a dubious distinction that begs the question, "What will Atlantic Yards look like in 20 years?"

Social scientists, economists, and ordinary citizens are debating the value of more mainstream-America additions to the urban fabric. Mill Harbor Waterview Residences at Bergen Beach near Mill Basin represent the first "gated" community in Brooklyn. Such closed solutions seem antithetical to New York's historic urban history. In another shift, big box retailing has already arrived, attracting SUVs and taxis and drawing apartment dwellers away from mom and pop stores on high streets.

Significant changes in shopping patterns have already transformed the monumental and commercial core of the former downtown. Today, a legal and educational center lies in proximity to 12 (!) subway lines, and downtown

Brooklyn (the third largest downtown in New York City, after Midtown and Lower Manhattan), boasts more than 75,000 workers and seven universities in proximity. Vibrant, funky retail action on the Fulton Street Mall ranks it among the top five such venues nationally, a situation that will only increase as more housing takes root. According to the *New York Times*, more than 7,000 housing units are currently in planning or in construction downtown. The city is instituting major changes that will improve streetscapes for clarity and create better pedestrian connections throughout the downtown.

As more towers ring the Civic Center and Metrotech, as housing rises along the riverfront, as new parklands emerge, and as the borough grows jumbo developments like Atlantic Yards, the question of Brooklyn's new persona inevitably arises. Will this place take on the hard-edged, decidedly impersonal character that comes with Manhattanization? Can or should we hang on to the singular flavor of the current approachable, dense urban agglomeration? If Brooklyn's hermetic independence as a city shifted throughout the 20th century, nevertheless its existing neighborhood structure is augmented by viable commercial, institutional, and recreational precincts in the current century that extend and amplify the opportunities for living and working in metropolitan New York. You can literally build a life there.

For this Brooklynite, who relishes propinquity (the recognition if not always the actual friendship of his neighbors: This is still New York), who feels sheltered by trees and streets and water and land, the defining question remains one of scale, humane scale, that early planners and builders got right, providing a framework for subsequent generations to weave their own culture and their own civilization within. My hope would be that in building for Brooklyn's future, we respect the pattern and use that framework to construct our own lives. Weekends I run on the bridge or in the park always with the anticipation of coming home. But in a decade, will Brooklyn still shelter me?

*ACKNOWLEDGMENTS*

I'd like to thank all the featured homeowners, architects, and designers for their thoughtful projects and willingness to talk about them. I'm also indebted to a few people whose work improved upon my text: valued designers and collaborators Emily CM Anderson, Adam Michaels, and Prem Krishnamurthy; photographer Yoko Inoue and assistants Daniel Dror and James Mahon; proofreader, Melissa Giannini; and as always, Rachel Somerstein.

First published in the United
States of America in 2008 by
Rizzoli International
Publications, Inc.
300 Park Avenue South
New York, NY 10010
www.rizzoliusa.com

2008 2009 2010 2011 /
10 9 8 7 6 5 4 3 2 1

Design by Project Projects
Printed in China

ISBN 10: 0-8478-3045-4
ISBN 13: 978-0-8478-3045-9

Library of Congress Catalog
Control Number: 2007905652